Manchester United —

1869 Newton Heath Railway Depot employees start having a bit of a kickabout amongst themselves.

1875 The Lancashire and Yorkshire Railway Cricket Club start a football section.

1878 First mention of Newton Heath Football Club playing at North Road, off Monsall Road.

1889 Newton Heath attempt to join the Football League — gaining only one vote. So they join the Football Alliance.

1891 Another attempt to join the Football League — this time they receive no votes.

1892 Football League splits into two divisions. Newton Heath join Division 1, with Ardwick (later becoming City) in Division 2.

1895 Newton Heath move to Bank Street, Clayton.

1896 Strip changes from green and gold to white shirts, blue shorts.

1902 Hard-up players pawn their suits to pay travelling expenses. Bankruptcy proceedings open for £2,670. John H. Davies, Director of Walker and Humphries, steps in and changes club's name to Manchester United.

1903 New red and white colours introduced.

1906 Promoted to the First Division with 62 points from 38 matches, scoring 90 goals.

1908 League Champions, partly due to 'poached' players.

1909 United win F.A. Cup for the first time, enabling J.H. Davies to afford £69,000 for a new ground at Old Trafford.

1910 19 February sees United's first game at Old Trafford — a 4-3 defeat by Liverpool.

1911 United win the League Championship for the second time.

1915 ⋯ n.

1921 ⋯ y.

1922

1924 ⋯ ts.

1925 ⋯ 0.

1931 United drop ⋯ :de 115 goals whilst gaining only 22 points.

1931 Christmas Eve and the club is broke. With no money for wages, the bank refuses to extend the overdraft. In steps James Gibson, Clothing firm Director, with £30,000.

1936 Back to the First Division with a new strip — white shirts with maroon V-loop. Immediately relegated.

1939 John Carey (£200 from Dublin), Jack Rowly (£3,000 from Bournemouth), Allenby Chilton and local-boy Stan Pearson help secure promotion.

1945 United emerge battered after the war, with no ground and some of its best players lost or retired.

1946 Ex-Sergeant Major Busby refuses jobs as Coach at Liverpool and Manager at Ayr United to join United for £15 per week.

1948 United win the F.A. Cup, the first major honour since 1911, with a 4-2 win over Blackpool.

1949 The fans come home to Old Trafford.

1952 After a long wait, United are Champions again.

1953 Matt Busby remarks to reporter Tom Jackson that seven first-team players are still teenagers. Manchester Evening News pictures them under "Busby Bloods his Babes" heading. A nickname is born and a new era started.

Newton Heath — Lancashire & Yorkshire Railway

FIRST TEAM.

DATE. 1886	NAME OF CLUB.	GROUND	GOALS. For Agt.
Aug. 28	Opening Game	Home..	
Sept. 4	Northwich Victoria	Home..	
,, 11	Oswaldtwistle Rovers	Home..	
,, 18	Stanley—Liverpool	Away..	won
,, 25	Hurst	Home..	lost
Oct. 2	Manchester	Home..	won
,, 9	Oswaldtwistle Rovers	Away..	draw
,, 16	Rawtenstall	Away..	
,, 23			
,, 30	1st round, E. C. T.		won
Nov. 6	Blackburn Olympic	Home..	
,, 13	Irwell Springs	Away..	lost
,, 20	Rawtenstall	Home..	draw
,, 27	Macclesfield	Home..	
Dec. 4	Manchester	Away..	won
,, 11	Hurst	Home..	
,, 18			
,, 25	Bury	Away..	
1887			
Jan. 1	Crewe Alexandra	Away..	
,, 8	Davenham	Away..	
,, 15	Irwell Springs	Home..	
,, 22	Witton	Home..	
,, 29	Stanley—Liverpool	Home..	
Feb. 5	Macclesfield	Away..	
,, 12	Bells' Temperance	Away..	
,, 19	M. & D. C. T.—1st round		
,, 26	2nd ,,		
Mar. 5			
,, 12			
,, 19	Davenham	Home..	
,, 26	Bells' Temperance	Home..	
Apl. 2			
,, 8	Good Friday.		
,, 9			
,, 16	Crewe Alexandra	Home..	
,, 23	Bury	Home..	
,, 30			

Newton Heath L.Y.R. Cricket and Football Club.

SEASON 1886-87.

President:

F. ATTOCK, ESQ.

Vice-Presidents:

Rt. Hon. Sir JAMES FERGUSSON, Bart., M.P.

C. E. SCHWANN, Esq., M.P.

C. P. SCOTT, Esq., J.P.   Mr. R. MORTON.

Dr. McDONALD.   Mr. J. HILTON.

Mr. J. HOWARTH.   Mr. W. WHITE.

Committee:

Mr. W. BLOW.	Mr. E. HINCHLEY.
Mr. J. COLLINSON.	Mr. T. JACKSON.
Mr. W. DOWNHILL.	Mr. S. JARRATT.
Mr. S. ECKERSLEY.	Mr. W. McCONNELL.
Mr. W. FRYAR.	Mr. J. PANTER.

Mr. T. RIGBY.

Captains:

Mr. J. POWELL (1st Team).

Mr. A. MACGREGOR (2nd Team—"Swifts.")

Financial Secretary:

Mr. Rd. ATHERTON, 451, Oldham-rd., Newton Heath.

Corresponding Secretary:

Mr. Jas. NEWALL, Dean Bank, Moston, Newton Heath.

DRESSING ROOM—"SHEARS HOTEL."

NOTE.—The present Cricket and Football year ends on April 30th, 1887, when all Subscriptions must be paid up.

COMELEY, PRINTER, BLUE BOAR COURT, MANCHESTER.

"SWIFTS" TEAM.

DATE. 1886	NAME OF CLUB.	GROUND	GOALS. For Agt.
Aug. 28			
Sept. 4	St. Helens 1st	Away..	
,, 11	Oswaldtwistle Rovers	Away..	
,, 18	Miles Platting 1st	Home..	
,, 25	Hurst Reserve	Home..	
Oct. 2	Manchester	Away..	
,, 9	Oswaldtwistle Rovers	Home..	
,, 16	Clifford 1st	Home..	
,, 23			
,, 30	West Gorton Athletic 1st	Home..	
Nov. 6			
,, 13			
,, 20	West Gorton Athletic 1st	Away..	
,, 27	Macclesfield Swifts	Away..	
Dec. 4	Manchester	Home..	
,, 11	Hurst Reserve	Away..	
,, 18	Bury	Home..	
,, 25			
1887			
Jan. 1	Crewe Hornets	Home..	
,, 8	Haughton 1st	Home..	
,, 15	Miles Platting 1st	Away..	
,, 22			
,, 29	Haughton 1st	Away..	
Feb. 5	Macclesfield Swifts	Home..	
,, 12			
,, 19			
,, 26			
Mar. 5	Clifford 1st	Away..	
,, 12			
,, 19	St. Helens	Away..	
,, 26			
Apl. 2			
,, 8	Good Friday.		
,, 9			
,, 16	Crewe Hornets	Away..	
,, 23	Bury	Away..	
,, 30			

SEASON 1886–7, MEMBERS ADMITTANCE CARD

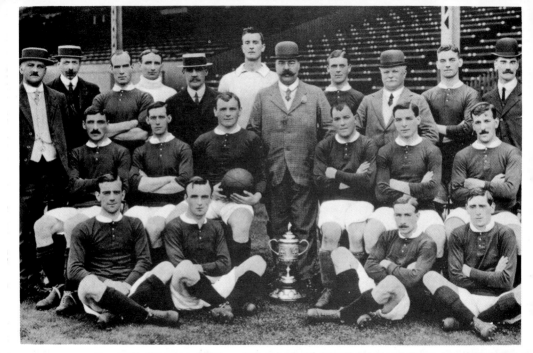

Memories
Football Memories: Manchester United (no.1)

F.A. CUP WINNERS, 1909.
Back: Ernest Mangnall (Manager/Secretary), Fred Bacon (Trainer), Jack Picken, Edmonds, Mr. McMurray*, Harry Moger,
John H. Davies**, T. Homer, Mr. G. Lawton*, Alex Bell, Mr. Deakin*;
Middle: Billy Meredith, Dick Duckworth, Charlie "The Ghost" Roberts, Sandy Turnball (the winning-goal scorer),
Enoch West, Stacey;
Front: Whalley, Hofton, Harold Halse, George Wall.   *Director, **Chairman

FOOTBALL - MANCHESTER UNITED PLAYERS

Memories

Football Memories: Manchester United (no.1)

NEARLY A THIRD DIVISION TEAM.
1933–34 saw United avoid relegation to Division Three
with a 2-0 win against Milwall at the Den in the final
game. This team included Jack Silcock, Tommy Jones,
Tommy Brean, George Vose and Jack Mellor.

POST CARD

FOR CORRESPONDENCE

FOR ADDRESS ONLY

Memories

Football Memories: Manchester United (no.1)

READY FOR ACTION, 1946–47.
United before a league match . . . without Johnny Carey?
Back: J. Warner, J. Roach, A. Chilton, C. Collinson,
B. Whalley, J. Aston;
Front: J. Delaney, S. Pearson, J. Hanlon, J. Rowley, C. Mitten.

FOR CORRESPONDENCE

FOR ADDRESS ONLY

Memories

Football Memories: Manchester United (no.1)

A 1948 LEAGUE LINE-UP.
Back: Jack Rowley, John Aston, Jack Crompton, Allenby
  Chilton, Stan Pearson, Billy McGlen;
Front: Jim Delaney, John Morris, Jack Warner, John Hanlon,
  Charlie Mitten.

POST CARD

FOR CORRESPONDENCE | FOR ADDRESS ONLY

Memories

Football Memories: Manchester United (no.1)

THE 1948 F.A. CUP WINNERS.
The 4-2 defeat of Blackpool is regarded by many as one
of the finest Wembley finals.
Back: J. Carey, J. Anderson, J. Crompton, A. Chilton,
  H. Cockburn, J. Aston;
Front: J. Delaney, J. Morris, J. Rowley, S. Pearson, C. Mitten.

POST CARD

FOR CORRESPONDENCE

FOR ADDRESS ONLY

Memories

Football Memories: Manchester United (no.1)

THE START OF AN ERA (Late 1946).
The newly signed Manager Matt Busby shakes hands with
John Carey, as Tony Dowe, John Hanlon, Allenby
Chilton, Stan Pearson, John Aston, John Warner,
Norman Tapkin and Ted Buckle look on.

Memories

Football Memories: Manchester United (no.1)

FIRST DIVISION CHAMPIONS, 1952.
The team which won the 1951–52 Championship and the
Charity Shield contained the first of the "Busby Babes"
— John Berry and Roger Byrne. As well as Johnny Carey
who left in 1953 after 344 games for United.

FOR CORRESPONDENCE | FOR ADDRESS ONLY

Memories

Football Memories: Manchester United (no.1)

THE "BUSBY BABES", 1957.
Back: W. McGuiness, D. Viollet, R. Charlton, J. Doherty, J. Blanchflower, A. Scanlon;
Middle: R. Wood, I. Greaves, W. Foulkes, F. Goodwin, L. Whelan, M. Jones, D. Edwards, G. Layton;
Front: C. Webster, J. Whitefoot, J. Berry, M. Busby, R. Byrne, T. Taylor, E. Colman, D. Pegg.

POST CARD

FOR CORRESPONDENCE | FOR ADDRESS ONLY

Memories
Football Memories: Manchester United (no.1)

F.A. CUP WINNERS, 1957.
Pictured in their special Cup strip before a training session, but Tommy Taylor is missing with flu.
Back: Tom Curry (Trainer), Duncan Edwards, Mark Jones, Ray Wood, Bobby Charlton, Bill Foulkes, Matt Busby;
Front: John Berry, Bill Whelan, Roger Byrne, David Pegg, Eddie Colman.

POST CARD

FOR CORRESPONDENCE

FOR ADDRESS ONLY

Memories

Football Memories: Manchester United (no.1)

CHRISTMAS, 1957.
Back: Edwards, Foulkes, Jones, Wood, Colman, Pegg;
Front: Berry, Whelan, Byrne, Taylor, Viollet.

POST CARD

FOR CORRESPONDENCE | FOR ADDRESS ONLY

Memories

Football Memories: Manchester United (no.1)

DUNCAN EDWARDS.
Shown here on his 21st birthday, Duncan was born on
1 October, 1936, He made his United debut at the age
of sixteen on 4 April, 1953, and was the youngest player
to be capped for England in April, 1955. He scored
nineteen goals in his 151 United appearances.

POST CARD

Memories
Football Memories: Manchester United (no.1)

UNITED REBUILT, 1958.
R. Charlton (inset)
Back: R. Harrop, I. Greaves, F. Goodwin, H. Gregg, S. Crowther, R. Cope, S. Brennan, W. Inglis (Assistant Trainer);
Front: J. Crompton (Trainer), A. Dawson, M. Pearson, W. Foulkes, E. Taylor, C. Webster.

POST CARD

FOR CORRESPONDENCE

FOR ADDRESS ONLY

Memories

Football Memories: Manchester United (no.1)

MANCHESTER UNITED, 1960–61.
Back: M. Setters, W. Foulkes, S. Brennan, H. Gregg,
 N. Cantwell, J. Nicholson;
Front: A. Quixall, N. Stiles, A. Dawson, M. Pearson, R. Charlton.

POST CARD

|

Memories
Football Memories: Manchester United (no.1)

THEY ALSO SERVE ...
The first team players backed by the Directors and various members of staff at the beginning of the 1960–61 season.
Front: J. Giles, M. Pearson, N. Stiles, F. Foulkes, N. Lawton, A. Quixall, R. Charlton, J. Crompton (Trainer), M. Setters.
 M. Busby, S. Brennan, H. Gregg, A. Dawson, N. Cantwell, D. Herd, D. Viollet

MANCHESTER UNITED F.C.

POST CARD

FOR CORRESPONDENCE | FOR ADDRESS ONLY

Memories
Football Memories: Manchester United (no.1)

F.A. CUP WINNERS, 1963.
Back: M. Setters, J. Nicholson, D. Gaskell, S. Brennan, M. Pearson, N. Cantwell;
Middle: W. Foulkes, S. McMillan, T. Dunne, N. Stiles, N. Lawton;
Front: J. Giles, A Quixall, D. Herd, D. Law, R. Charlton.

POST CARD

FOR CORRESPONDENCE

FOR ADDRESS ONLY

Memories

Football Memories: Manchester United (no.1)

LEAGUE CHAMPIONS, 1964–65.
This was the start of a consistent run culminating in the European Cup win in 1968.
Back: N. Stiles, T. Dunne, D. Gaskell, P. Dunne, P. Crerand, J. Fitzpatrick;
Middle: S. Brennan, D. Saddler, W. Foulkes, J. Aston, N. Cantwell;
Front: J. Connelly, R. Charlton, D. Herd, D. Law, G. Best.

POST CARD

FOR CORRESPONDENCE

FOR ADDRESS ONLY

Memories

Football Memories: Manchester United (no.1)

DENIS LAW.
Born on 24 February, 1940, in Aberdeen, Denis joined
United for a then record £115,000 from Turin in July,
1962. He scored 171 goals in 309 games for United,
before moving to Maine Road on a free transfer in 1973.

POST CARD

Memories

Football Memories: Manchester United (no.1)

BOBBY CHARLTON.
Born 11 October, 1937, Bobby scored twice on his debut
as United beat Charlton Athletic 4-2 on 6 October, 1956.
He scored 199 goals in 604 games for United, and 49 goals
whilst gaining 106 England caps.

POST CARD

FOR CORRESPONDENCE

FOR ADDRESS ONLY

Memories

Football Memories: Manchester United (no.1)

SIR MATT BUSBY.
Matt pictured with the Central League Trophy which United
won in 1955–56.

POST CARD

Memories

Football Memories: Manchester United (no.1)

GEORGE BEST.
Born 22 May, 1946, in Belfast, George made his United debut against West Brom on 14 September, 1963. He scored 137 goals, playing the last of his 361 games for United on New Years Day, 1974.

FOR CORRESPONDENCE

FOR ADDRESS ONLY

Memories

Football Memories: Manchester United (no.1)

EUROPEAN CUP WINNERS, 1968.
Back: W. Foulkes, J. Aston, J. Rimmer, A. Stepney, A. Gowling, D. Herd;
Middle: D. Sadler, A. Dunne, S. Brennan, P. Crerand, G. Best, F. Burns, J. Crompton (Trainer);
Front: J. Ryan, N. Stiles, D. Law, M. Busby (Manager), R. Charlton, B. Kidd, J. Fitzpatrick.

Memories

Football Memories: Manchester United (no.1)

BOUNCE STRAIGHT BACK.
This United squad played just the one season, 1974–75, in the Second Division.
Back: T. Docherty (Manager), S. Houston, S. James, P. Roche, A. Stepney, A. Sidebottom, J. Holton, M. Buchan, P. Bielby,
   T. Cavanagh (Trainer);
Front: M. Martin, S. McIlroy, A. Forsyth, B. Greenhoff, W. Morgan, T. Anderson, J. McCalliog, L. Macari, G. Daly, A. Young.